Kamil Idris

DEMYSTIFY
THE UNSEEN PATH

U K

First published in Great Britain in 2024

Editing, design, typesetting and publishing by UK Book Publishing.

www.ukbookpublishing.com

ISBN: 978-1-917329-33-0

Contents

"To those in search of divine wisdom, true knowledge and the value of patience"

Prologue

Throughout the extensive timeline of human history, there are stories that surpass cultural, religious and temporal limits, striking a chord with the shared consciousness of humanity. One such enduring tale is the mysterious meeting between Moses, a respected prophet in Abrahamic faiths and Al Khidr, a figure veiled in enigma and deep insight. Despite its brevity, their encounter symbolizes the timeless pursuit of wisdom, comprehension and spiritual awakening.

"Demystify: The Unseen Path" aims to delve into the captivating tale, revealing its significance and revelations. Setting off on this journey encourages us to engage in the lessons of the intricacies of human thought and the transformative impact of stepping into uncharted territories. The narrative of Moses and Al Khidr goes beyond legend; it serves as a reflection showcasing truths that still influence our lives in the present day.

The Enigmatic Figures:

Moses, a known figure in history, is celebrated for his leadership, unwavering faith and strong bond with the divine. His journey, from the banks of the Nile to the peak of Mount Sinai, illustrates his pursuit of truth and justice. Despite his stature Moses humbly recognizes the limits of his knowledge. It is his humility and ongoing thirst for knowledge that drive him to seek out Al Khidr, a figure known for wisdom that transcends understanding.

Al Khidr, also referred to as "The Green One", represents wisdom and everlasting existence in beliefs. He is highly respected and shrouded in mystery, embodying the knowledge that surpasses understanding. Through his sometimes-contradictory deeds, Al Khidr questions traditional views, on right and wrong, providing insights into the mechanisms of the cosmos.

The Meeting and Its Significance:

The meeting of Moses and Al Khidr takes place amidst a context of exploration and heavenly guidance. As per the Quranic account, Moses sets off on a voyage, with Al Khidr's guidance. This expedition is characterized by a sequence of occurrences that challenge Moses's comprehension, testing his endurance and belief.

From the start, Al Khidr makes it clear that Moses needs to be patient and hold back from asking questions about his actions until the reasons behind them are made known. This requirement lays the groundwork for a dive into themes like trust, modesty and the essence of wisdom. Every incident during their travels, starting with the boat incident, to the boy's death and ending with the wall being rebuilt, prompts contemplation and insight.

The Lessons of the Journey:

The tale of Moses and Al Khidr is filled with insights that resonate with the essence of existence. It shows us that genuine wisdom is not always evident, at a glance urging us to be patient and have faith in order to grasp its meaning. The harmful deeds of Al Khidr serve a cause in highlighting the intricacies of divine justice and the boundaries of human understanding.

1. Patience and Trust:

The story underscores the significance of having patience and faith when seeking wisdom. Moses's impatience at first, followed by his realization, showcases the importance of enduring doubt. Having trust in the journey. This message holds relevance in a society that frequently seeks fixes and instant solutions.

2. Humility and Openness:

The story emphasizes the importance of humility. Moses, even though he is a prophet, shows humility by approaching Al Khidr and admitting his desire for knowledge. This act of humility allows for insight and personal development, highlighting that regardless of our accomplishments there is always room to expand our understanding.

3. Complexity of Justice:

Al Khidr's actions challenge conventional notions of fairness, revealing a deep and complex understanding of divine wisdom. The narrative presents a nuanced view on ethical dilemmas, recognizing that what appears unjust initially could serve a greater purpose.

4. Embracing Uncertainty:

The narrative encourages us to welcome the facets of life with belief and strength. Acknowledging that certain truths may escape our grasp empowers us to face obstacles, with confidence and reliance, with assistance.

The Timeless Relevance:

The tale of Moses and Al Khidr transcends any era or location; its teachings hold relevance across all ages. In a time characterized by transformations, ethical grey areas and profound existential questions, this story provides wisdom for navigating the intricacies of modern day existence.

1. Lifelong Learning:

The meeting emphasized the importance of learning and that of personal growth. Embodying a state of mind leads to broadening of our comprehension, and to facing difficulties with more flexibility towards them.

2. Holistic Perspective:

Al Khidr's actions showcase how everything and everyone are connected, promoting an approach to decision making. This approach is crucial for tackling issues, like protecting the environment, ensuring fairness and reducing economic disparities.

3. Balancing Reason and Faith:

The story emphasizes the importance of combining questioning with belief and confidence. This harmony encourages a perspective, on comprehending the world, blending thinking with intuitive wisdom.

4. Compassion and Justice:

Trying to strike a balance between understanding and justice in our actions can positively influence the well-being of those around us. This sense of balance plays a role in decision making and building relationships.

A Journey for All Seekers:

"Demystify: The Unseen Path" encourages readers to set out on their quest for knowledge, drawing inspiration from the accounts of Moses and Al Khidr. Whether you are delving into insights, wrestling with quandaries or pursuing self-improvement, their expedition imparts meaningful advice and motivation.

As we delve into the narrative, we are reminded that acquiring wisdom is not an endeavour but a collective voyage experienced by all individuals. The story encourages us to seek guidance from mentors, embrace life's hurdles, and maintain trust in the acquisition of wisdom. Reflecting on the experiences of Moses and Al Khidr, we find inspiration to navigate our journeys with humility, perseverance and faith.

Conclusion:

In the faint glow of age-old stories, the tale of Moses and Al Khidr stands out as a source of profound insight and motivation. It goes beyond religious and cultural divides, imparting enduring teachings that touch upon the core of human nature. As we delve into "Demystify: The Unseen Path", we are encouraged to delve into the profound wisdom of the divine, embrace the enigmas of life, and believe in the profound impact of seeking transformation.

May this adventure motivate us to develop patience, modesty and faith, in our lives. Let us discover the bravery to welcome unpredictability and the intelligence to acknowledge the interdependence of all living creatures. May we stay receptive to the advice and revelations that arise from our encounters, enabling them to change and enhance our perception of the world and ourselves.

Chapter 1

The Quest for Knowledge

Moses, a figure in the faiths, is celebrated not just for his guidance and prophetic duties but also for his relentless quest for knowledge. His encounter with Al Khidr commences with a question that resonates with many: How can we achieve wisdom? This section delves into the reasons driving Moses's pursuit, the historical backdrop of his era and the lasting significance of his exploration, in today's world.

The Drive for Knowledge:

Moses's choice to look for Al Khidr is fuelled by a sense of humility and awareness of his limitations. With his guidance and achievements, Moses understands that his knowledge is not all-encompassing. This recognition marks the stage in the pursuit of knowledge; it signifies the understanding that genuine wisdom starts with acknowledging our gaps in knowledge. This humility isn't a display of weakness. It showcases Moses's strength and willingness to evolve.

In today's world this teaching holds significance. We are surrounded by a wealth of information, in the age within reach. Yet amidst this abundance true comprehension can sometimes be clouded. Moses's journey serves as a reminder that acquiring knowledge demands insight, modesty and a readiness to seek wisdom beyond what's readily available to us.

Historical and Cultural Context:

To truly understand Moses's journey, we need to take into account the cultural setting of his era. Moses existed during a time of social change. His task to free the Israelites from slavery, in Egypt, and guide them to the Promised Land was filled with obstacles. The backdrop of hardship and change emphasizes the importance of his search for insight.

The tale of Moses and Al Khidr unfolds within a rich tapestry of age-old customs and tales that underscore the quest for knowledge as a revered and crucial pursuit. Across various ancient societies like the Egyptians and Mesopotamians, who left their mark on the Israelites, wisdom held great significance and was frequently depicted as a divine quality. Moses is following a timeless tradition of seeking enlightenment in search of Al Khidr.

The Significance of Al Khidr:

Al Khidr, known as "The Green One", is a figure highly respected for his wisdom. According to beliefs, Al Khidr is considered a saint with insights into the unknown and who follows divine guidance. He serves not as a mentor in the tale. But he represents a profound wisdom that goes beyond traditional knowledge.

Moses's search for Al Khidr symbolizes his longing to surpass the boundaries of wisdom and uncover the realities of life. This expedition isn't merely an excursion but a spiritual exploration that demands Moses to venture outside his territory and welcome uncertainty. It reflects our endeavour to make sense of life's intricacies and uncertainties, in a world filled with complexities.

The Courage to Seek:

Moses demonstrates a great amount of bravery and persistence, in his quest. Choosing to search for Al Khidr means stepping from the known and delving into territory. This element of his adventure highlights the notion that the pursuit of knowledge is a task for those with courage. It demands facing ambiguity, questioning beliefs and staying receptive to occasionally unsettling realities.

In today's world courage plays a role. Seeking knowledge often requires challenging existing beliefs, pushing boundaries and venturing into territories. Whether in the fields of science, philosophy or self-improvement, having the bravery to pursue and accept information is key to advancement and personal growth.

Lessons for Today:

Moses's search for knowledge teaches us lessons that remain relevant today. It emphasizes the significance of humility in the journey towards wisdom. Genuine wisdom starts with acknowledging our limitations and being open to learning from those with insight.

Secondly, Moses's adventure showcases the significance of bravery and perseverance when facing challenges. Exploring territories and embracing the unknown are steps in the pursuit of knowledge. Courage, resilience and a steadfast dedication to honesty are qualities for success.

Finally, Moses's journey serves as a reminder of the enduring pursuit of wisdom. Across generations the thirst for knowledge has been an aspect of society. By emulating the paths of revered individuals such as Moses and Al Khidr, we uphold a legacy. Seek to unveil the profound truths that shape our very being.

In summary, Moses's pursuit of knowledge is a motivating adventure that resonates with the essence of existence. This journey urges us to embody humility, bravery and perseverance as we strive for wisdom in our lives. As we face the intricacies of today's world let us find motivation in Moses's story and persist in uncovering the truths that guide our way.

Chapter 2

The Mysterious Guide

Al Khidr, a wise figure, played a role in Moses's journey. Referred to as "The Green One", Al Khidr symbolizes life, wisdom and hidden cosmic knowledge. This section explores the persona of Al Khidr, his representation in teachings, and the profound symbolism he represents. Through unravelling the essence of Al Khidr, we uncover insights into guidance and its impact on our lives.

Al Khidr in Islamic Tradition:

In Islamic culture Al Khidr is commonly seen as a saint or prophet, with an existence, even though there is uncertainty surrounding his true essence. It is believed that he has been bestowed with insights by God, enabling him to understand and respond to realities of the universe. The story of Al Khidr in the Quran detailed in Surah Al Kahf (18;60-82) depicts him as a servant of God who teaches Moses profound lessons, through actions that may seem inexplicable.

The idea of Al Khidr's life is a motif in different cultures, indicating that he exists beyond the usual boundaries of time and space. This characteristic underscores the nature of insight which is unrestricted by human limitations. Al Khidr's wisdom and deeds may sometimes seem puzzling or conflicting to our minds, underscoring the contrast between knowledge and human comprehension.

The Symbolism of Al Khidr:

Al Khidr's clothing and connection to lush imagery represent vitality, rejuvenation and progress. The colour green, often associated with the world and energy, symbolizes the circle of life and the everlasting flow of divine wisdom. This symbolism highlights Al Khidr's position as a mentor who fosters development and understanding.

Al Khidr's actions, which left Moses perplexed, serve as a reminder that divine wisdom operates in ways that surpass our comprehension. His enigmatic ways urge us to embrace life's intricacies and recognize that certain truths transcend understanding. Through his nature, Al Khidr encourages us to trust in the wisdom guiding our paths when it appears puzzling at first.

The Role of Al Khidr as a Guide:

Al Khidr plays a role, as a mentor and tester, for Moses. He takes Moses through challenges to show the constraints of perception and the importance of divine wisdom. Al Khidr's guidance focuses on sparking introspection and comprehension, rather than offering direct solutions.

Al Khidr, as a mentor figure, represents traits like patience, wisdom and intuition. He makes decisions with a sense of purpose and understanding of the picture, even if they seem confusing to Moses. This aspect of Al Khidr's persona underscores the significance of having faith, in the learning and development process. Genuine guidance often requires us to navigate ambiguity and welcome the unfamiliar, believing that the path will ultimately lead to insights.

Lessons from Al Khidr's Guidance:

The interactions, between Al Khidr and Moses, offer perspectives on the importance of guidance and wisdom:

1. Patience and Humility:

In order for Moses to join Al Khidr, he must show patience and refrain from questioning Al Khidr's actions. This condition highlights the significance of being patient and humble while seeking knowledge. Gaining wisdom often involves setting aside our preconceptions and being willing to learn from situations that may challenge our beliefs.

2. Seeing Beyond Appearances:

Al Khidr's behaviour, like causing damage to the boat or taking the life of the boy, may seem severe and unfair at glance. Yet each action is eventually shown to have a reason that contributes to a higher cause. This message encourages us to see beyond surface appearances and take into account the aspects of situations. It serves as a reminder that the truth behind events is frequently intricate, requiring us to explore for genuine comprehension.

3. The Role of Divine Wisdom:

Al Khidr is believed to possess wisdom that comes from an origin highlighting the difference between intelligence and divine insight. Human knowledge is limited. It can be mistaken, while divine wisdom offers a perspective beyond our understanding. This lesson emphasizes the importance of faith and trusting in a power, recognizing that some truths are beyond our grasp.

4. *The Journey of Learning:*

Al Khidr's teachings evolve continuously mirroring the changing nature of the learning journey. Genuine wisdom is not a stop, but a perpetual journey of development and exploration. The exchanges between Al Khidr and Moses demonstrate that seeking knowledge is a commitment that demands determination and a receptive spirit.

Contemporary Relevance:

In today's world, the teachings from Al Khidr's guidance still hold significance. As we tackle the intricacies of life, we encounter moments that test our knowledge and push us to acknowledge our boundaries. Al Khidr's tale encourages us to meet these trials with patience, modesty and a readiness to have faith in the wisdom that underlies them.

In today's era the quest for knowledge can feel daunting, given the amount of information easily accessible to us. Al Khidr's story serves as a reminder that genuine wisdom goes beyond amazing facts; it involves delving into comprehension and perception. It inspires us to nurture a spirit of awe and inquisitiveness, welcoming life's enigmas of expecting solutions.

In addition, the tale of Al Khidr underscores the significance of having mentors and guidance in both our professional spheres. Similar to how Moses approached Al Khidr, we can also reap rewards by seeking out mentors who have wisdom and experience. By absorbing lessons from those who have tread the path before us, we can acquire perspectives and steer our own paths with enhanced understanding and direction.

In conclusion, the enigmatic mentorship of Al Khidr imparts teachings on wisdom, patience, humility and trust in the pursuit of knowledge. His narrative urges us to see beyond surface impressions, accept life's intricacies, and strive for comprehension. As we ponder Al Khidr's counsel, may it motivate us to embark on our journeys with bravery, inquisitiveness and a receptive spirit.

Chapter 3

The Journey Begins

Moses travels with Al Khidr, representing an exploration of curiosity, towards spiritual enlightenment and the transformative impacts it brings. This segment delves into the phase of their journey, emphasizing the significance of the obstacles they face and the valuable lessons embedded in these trials. As Moses embarks on this quest, he is challenged to transcend his beliefs and embrace an understanding of the divine wisdom shaping existence.

The Agreement and the Conditions:

The adventure starts with Moses and Al Khidr reaching an understanding. Moses shares his eagerness to gain knowledge from Al Khidr, who in turn advises Moses to be patient and not inquire about his actions until he decides to reveal the reasons behind them. This arrangement establishes the mood for the expedition, highlighting the significance of patience, modesty and faith, in the learning experience.

In this story patience plays a role in representing the importance of enduring ambiguity and avoiding judgments. Moses, a prophet used to receiving instructions, finds this situation particularly challenging. He must let go of control and embrace wisdom, believing that clarity will eventually emerge.

The Symbolism of the Journey:

The adventure Moses and Al Khidr embark on symbolizes the path each individual must follow in pursuit of wisdom. It entails venturing beyond boundaries and delving into territories at times. This expedition signifies a transition, from perceiving the world to comprehending the core principles that influence our being.

As Moses and Al Khidr journey side by side, the route they take symbolizes the phases of growth. Every meeting and occurrence they come across acts as a teaching moment, slowly revealing the depths of insight and prompting Moses to broaden his outlook.

The First Trial: The Breaking of the Boat:

The first pivotal moment of the journey was when their boat broke down. Moses and Al Khidr hopped on a boat offered by villagers. Al Khidr intentionally damaged it, rendering it unfit for sailing. This surprising action left Moses puzzled and prompted him to question Al Khidr going against their understanding.

Al Khidr's reaction to Moses's impatience serves as a reminder of the importance of waiting for all the details to emerge before passing judgment. Even though breaking the boat may seem damaging, there is a reason behind it that Moses is not able to grasp at the moment.

The Symbolism of the Boat:

The boat serves as a source of sustenance and livelihood, for the villagers embodying the tangible assistance and assurance that individuals depend on for their well-being. Al Khidr's action of harming the boat may be interpreted as symbolizing the disturbance of material security to uncover realities.

This event shows Moses, and also the reader, that divine wisdom works in mysterious ways. What seems like harm or destruction might actually be for a greater good that isn't obvious at first. It makes us question the idea that suffering or loss is always a bad thing, proposing instead that these experiences can bring about spiritual growth and enlightenment.

The Second Trial: The Killing of the Boy:

The second pivotal moment that unfolds sparks inquiries when Al Khidr comes across a boy. For mysterious reasons he brings an end to his life. This incident greatly troubles Moses, leading him to seek clarification from Al Khidr as he struggles to understand the reasoning behind such a deed.

Al Khidr's reaction serves as a nudge to encourage patience and discourage questioning. This event challenges Moses's beliefs and knowledge, urging him to explore the boundaries of his understanding.

The Symbolism of the Boy:

The boy symbolizes purity and promise, which adds complexity to the struggle of finding meaning in his passing. From one perspective the boy's death may serve as a metaphor for the unfathomable nature of divine retribution. This provokes contemplation on ideas of right and wrong, hinting at truths beyond our grasp.

This trial underscores the significance of trusting in guidance even when it contradicts beliefs and emotions. It demonstrates to Moses that true wisdom entails accepting life's facets, when they defy comprehension.

The Third Trial: The Restoration of the Wall:

The last important occurrence, during their journey, involves fixing a deteriorating wall in a town where the locals are unwelcoming. Even though the residents do not show any hospitality, Al Khidr decides to repair the wall without expecting anything in return, leaving Moses puzzled.

Moses raises doubts about the reasons behind this act of kindness despite facing hostility, but Al Khidr uncovers the intention: there is a treasure beneath the wall that belongs to two orphaned boys. By fixing the wall, Al Khidr ensures that the treasure stays safe until the boys are old enough to discover it.

The Symbolism of the Wall:

The wall stands as a shield and keeper, embodying the gifts and heavenly safeguard present in our world. Al Khidr's decision to rebuild the wall in the face of the villagers' lack of gratitude showcases the idea of unwavering kindness and the divine watch over us that transcends actions.

Moses learns from this occurrence that divine wisdom includes both compassion and foresight, sometimes appearing in ways that are not immediately clear to humans. It underscores the notion that gestures of kindness and protection may have effects extending beyond what meets the eye.

The Revelation of Wisdom:

Upon reaching the end of their journey, Al Khidr reveals the motivations behind his deeds, offering Moses the background. Every action, though appearing confusing and unfair at glance, serves a grander design in line with understanding. This disclosure serves as a moment of enlightenment for Moses, highlighting the boundaries of insight and emphasizing the importance of having faith in a superior wisdom.

Al Khidr's explanations highlight the equilibrium of fairness, empathy and foresight in actions. They underscore that genuine wisdom considers not the outcomes, but also the far-reaching effects on both individuals and communities.

Lessons for Contemporary Life:

Moses's early experiences, alongside Al Khidr, provide insights that are relevant to our modern lives:

1. Patience and Trust:

The decision to stay patient and avoid asking questions underscores the significance of trust in the educational journey. In a society that frequently seeks solutions, this teaching serves as a reminder to welcome ambiguity and have faith in the gradual development of knowledge.

2. Deeper Understanding:

The trials endured by Moses motivates us to look away from superficial meanings, and into deep ones. They are constantly reminding us that there's more to what meets the eye. Something that appears to be negative at a first glance, may have a meaningful purpose in the pursuit of personal growth and progress.

3. Compassion and Foresight:

The actions of Al Khidr show us the value of compassion and that of foresight towards the guidance of our actions and words. They remind us to look at the deeper implications of our decision-making process, to act with kindness, care and purpose, even when it is not reciprocated straight away.

4. Acceptance of Mystery:

The voyage highlights the importance of embracing the enigmas of life. It prompts us to recognize the boundaries of our comprehension, and to stay receptive to the insight that functions beyond our awareness.

Ultimately, the start of Moses's adventure with Al Khidr symbolizes a metaphor for the search for enlightenment. It urges us to welcome patience, faith and a deeper grasp of the laws that shape our existence. As we ponder the teachings from their expedition, may we discover motivation to navigate our journeys, with modesty, empathy and a steadfast dedication to seeking wisdom.

Chapter 4

The Breaking of the Boat

Moses and Al Khidr's meeting takes a turn when Al Khidr causes harm to a boat owned by villagers. This act, which may appear destructive at first, carries symbolism. It imparts valuable lessons on divine wisdom, the importance of patience, and the need to have faith in a greater purpose. In this chapter we delve into the meanings of this incident, exploring how it shapes Moses's path and its wider significance, for our lives.

The Context of the Act:

Moses and Al Khidr set sail on a boat offered by villagers who graciously lend their vessel for the journey. While on board, Al Khidr unexpectedly damages the boat by creating a hole in its hull, leaving Moses puzzled by this detrimental act. In response to this incident, Moses breaks his silence and patience, questioning Al Khidr about his actions.

Moses's response makes sense. In his view the action seems unfair and illogical, putting the villagers' well-being at risk despite their kindness. This quick reaction shows how humans often assess situations based on what they see on the surface and their own limited knowledge.

The Symbolism of the Boat:

The boat is a symbol for the villagers representing security, sustenance and the livelihood of the community. It embodies the resources for survival and maintaining stability. In this context the boat serves as a metaphor for the pillars of support in our lives, encompassing our careers, connections, with others and material belongings.

Al Khidr's decision to damage the boat questions the belief that material stability is consistently advantageous. This action prompts a reassessment of what defines security and prosperity. Through damaging the boat, Al Khidr initiates a moment that leads to a significance, unveiling profound insights into divine wisdom and human comprehension.

The Necessity of Disruption:

Upon observation, the actions of Al Khidr may seem destructive at first. Yet as the narrative progresses it becomes evident that this disruption serves a purpose, in averting a significant danger. In a revelation Al Khidr clarifies that he intentionally harmed the boat to protect it from being taken by a ruler who was seizing all seaworthy vessels. Through this setback, Al Khidr secures the enduring well-being of the boat and the livelihood of its owners.

This story illustrates that not all disruptions are negative; some are essential to prevent setbacks or achieve a benefit. It challenges the notion that stability and predictability are always advantageous, suggesting that periods of transition can lead to adaptability and understanding.

Patience and Trust in Divine Wisdom:

One important takeaway from this situation is the value of being patient and having faith when dealing with situations. Moses's initial response, to questioning Al Khidr's decisions, demonstrates an inclination to want quick answers and solutions. Nevertheless, genuine wisdom often calls for patience and the capacity to reserve judgment until the full picture becomes clear.

Al Khidr's request for Moses to practise patience and avoid questioning highlights the importance of having faith in wisdom. This faith involves more than accepting things as they are, but also involves embracing the unknown, acknowledging that our understanding is limited and cannot fully grasp divine plans. It serves as a reminder to have faith and trust that every situation when it seems confusing has a meaning behind it.

The Role of Suffering and Loss:

The boat breaking incident also reflects on how suffering and loss shape experiences. Looking at it spiritually, times of loss and upheaval can bring about transformation, offering chances for development and a deeper insight. Although the initial damage to the boat was distressing and unnerving, it ended up safeguarding the villagers from a calamity.

This teaching holds significance during challenging moments. It proposes that enduring hardship though tough can result in changes that may not be apparent anyway. It motivates people to find purpose in their trials and to stay receptive to the idea that obstacles can trigger individual development.

Lessons for Contemporary Life:

The incident involving the boat breaking provides insights on how to navigate the challenges of modern-day life:

1. Embracing Change and Disruption:

The narrative prompts us to see disruptions, not as occurrences but as chances, for personal development and change. It proposes that times of uncertainty can foster resilience and insight, equipping us to face obstacles.

2. Patience and Long-term Perspective:

The importance of being patient when dealing with uncertainty is a lesson to learn. In today's fast-paced society where quick answers and fixes are often expected, this tale serves as a reminder of the significance of taking a long-term view and having faith in a plan.

3. Reevaluating Material Security:

The boat's symbolism questions the idea that relying on material stability is advantageous. It prompts us to explore the underlying foundations of security and happiness, advocating for a shift towards personal strength, rather than just material wealth.

4. Finding Meaning in Suffering:

The story implies that facing difficulties and conquering obstacles can result in changes. It motivates people to find significance in their struggles and stay receptive to the possibility of evolving amidst turbulent times.

The Broader Implications:

The tale of the boat's destruction holds meanings for grasping the essence of wisdom and the human experience. It underscores how our perception can be misguided, and the importance of relying on an intelligence that shapes the world. This reliance isn't belief but a thoughtful acknowledgment of our own constraints and the boundless intricacies of the divine scheme.

The story also highlights how events are connected and how one person's actions can have far-reaching effects. Despite Al Khidr's action, at first it ends up leading to a positive outcome, showing how our lives are shaped by a complex interplay of causes and consequences. It promotes a perspective on life, acknowledging that every choice we make has repercussions that go beyond what we can grasp.

Conclusion:

The moment when the boat breaks during Moses and Al Khidr's journey is an event that teaches us lessons about divine wisdom, patience and how disruptions can lead to personal and spiritual growth. This story encourages us to see beyond the surface, have faith in a plan and recognize the power of hardship and setbacks. Let's use this narrative as inspiration to face our paths with belief, strength and an open mind, knowing that every obstacle plays a part in the scheme of divine wisdom.

Chapter 5

The Killing of the Boy

The incident where Al Khidr kills the boy is a morally complex moment in Moses's journey. This harsh and bewildering act pushes Moses – and by extension us as readers – to grapple with the deep intricacies of divine wisdom and justice. This chapter thoroughly explores the thematic importance of this event, delving into its impact on our perceptions of morality, fate and the role of intervention.

The Context of the Act:

During their travels, Al Khidr and Moses come across a boy. In a turn of events Al Khidr unexpectedly takes the boy's life, leaving Moses shocked and bewildered by the act. This starkly contrasts with the perception of intervention, prompting immediate reflections on justice and the moral implications of Al Khidr's behaviour.

Moses's response is a reaction to what seems like a severe act of violence. His instant disapproval of Al Khidr's behaviour shows an instinct to defend the innocent and denounce unfair harm. This incident acts as a trial of Moses's faith and comprehension, questioning his existing beliefs about what's right and just.

The Symbolism of the Boy:

The boy represented purity, optimism and a positive mindset for what is yet to come. His spirit reflected the endless promising days for children. His death serves as a touching reminder of how nothing is permanent. It motivates us to realise that life sometimes takes turns we might not understand from where we are currently standing.

This particular incident also delves into the idea of fate and predestination. The death of the boy, as later disclosed by Al Khidr is not an act of violence but a purposeful intervention based on foresight. It was the boy's destiny to evolve into someone who would bring about harm and suffering, and his untimely demise averts this future disaster. This storyline questions the often-oversimplified comprehension of life and death, introducing an intricate blend of destiny, choice and divine intent.

The Necessity of Divine Intervention:

Al Khidr's reasoning behind the act of killing highlights a key element of wisdom: the capability to perceive and respond to the impacts of actions that remain unseen by ordinary individuals. Al Khidr discloses that allowing the boy to live would have led to him becoming a tyrant inflicting hardship on his parents and community. Through his intervention, at that moment Al Khidr averts a fraught situation with increased malevolence and suffering.

Moses is challenged by this viewpoint to confront the concept that divine intervention, though it may appear severe or unfair at first, could ultimately lead to a purpose that surpasses understanding. It highlights the belief that divine wisdom takes into account a perspective of life, focusing not on instant results but considering the long term impacts of actions, over time and distance.

Moral and Ethical Implications:

The boy's death brings up moral dilemmas regarding justice and the influence of divine intervention on human matters. Looking at it from one perspective, purposefully ending the life of an innocent is a wrongdoing. Yet when viewed through the lens of understanding unjust deeds it might fulfil a greater purpose beyond typical moral boundaries.

This occasion questions the view of right and wrong, hinting that deeds should be judged through a perspective of spiritual wisdom. It prompts a reassessment of beliefs, proposing that genuine fairness necessitates grasping the intricate web of life's connections and the possible outcomes of choices.

Trust in Divine Wisdom:

One important takeaway from this incident is the importance of having faith in wisdom when it goes against our human reasoning. Moses's initial shock and doubt are reactions to what appears to be a harsh action. Yet Al Khidr's later explanation uncovers a deeper truth that Moses couldn't grasp by himself.

This tale explores the limits of how we perceive things and the importance of faith in a higher power. It suggests that understanding operates on a level that goes beyond logic, requiring a belief that goes deeper than what meets the eye. This belief goes beyond accepting; it involves embracing the mysteries of life and recognizing that our understanding is always incomplete and evolving.

Lessons for Contemporary Life:

The death of the boy provides insights into how we can tackle the moral and ethical challenges we face in today's world:

1. Embracing Complexity:

The tale urges us to accept the intricacies of ethical choices, understanding that our actions can lead to consequences that may not be obvious at first. It promotes a comprehension of justice that surpasses moral evaluations.

2. Trust in a Higher Plan:

The importance of having faith in the wisdom of a higher power is a lesson. In a world marred by pain and unfairness, this tale serves as a reminder to have confidence in the existence of a grander scheme that surpasses our comprehension.

3. The Role of Suffering:

The story implies that dealing with difficulties and barriers, though difficult, can be valuable, in acquiring insight. It urges people to discover significance in their challenges and stay receptive to the idea that obstacles can result in a comprehension and development on a higher level.

4. Reevaluating Justice:

The narrative prompts a reassessment of ideas of fairness, suggesting that justice necessitates grasping the intricate web of connections in life and the possible repercussions of decisions. It promotes a perspective on ethics that takes into account not just immediate results but also enduring effects.

The Broader Implications:

The boy's death has implications for how we perceive wisdom and the human experience. It emphasizes the boundaries of our understanding and the importance of having faith in an intelligence that shapes the world. This belief isn't trust but a thoughtful acknowledgment of our limitations and the intricate nature of a divine design.

The story also highlights how events are linked and how one action can have an effect. Although Al Khidr's initial actions seemed negative, they ended up leading to an outcome showing how every decision we make can impact the world around us. It promotes an understanding of life, acknowledging that our choices have far-reaching consequences that may not always be immediately clear.

Conclusion:

The tragic death of the child presents a thought-provoking dilemma, in the tale of Moses and Al Khidr. It compels us to grapple with the aspects of guidance, the concept of fairness, and the importance of faith in facing moral dilemmas. As we ponder over this narrative, let us gather the bravery to accept life's enigmas with modesty, endurance and an empathetic spirit, believing that each trial plays a part in revealing wisdom's design.

Chapter 6

The Restoration of the Wall

The last important occurrence, in the adventure of Moses and Al Khidr, revolves around repairing a deteriorating wall in a town. This act of kindness contrasts sharply with the destructive and aggressive deeds, imparting a deep lesson on the harmony between creation and destruction, empathy and the mysterious ways of divine insight. This section delves into the symbolism and underlying significance of this deed, exploring its impact on Moses's comprehension and its wider implications for our existence.

The Context of the Act:

After seeing the boat break and the boy being killed, Moses and Al Khidr reach a town, seeking shelter but are instead faced with hostility and rejection. Despite the unwelcoming reception, Al Khidr spots a crumbling wall and chooses to fix it. Moses, puzzled by this act of kindness towards their hosts, once more questions Al Khidr's motives.

Moses's reaction exemplifies the response to situations. Despite the lack of kindness from the villagers, Al Khidr's actions shed light on perspectives regarding fairness and empathy.

The Symbolism of the Wall:

The wall stands as a symbol of safety, conservation and the hidden blessings that nurture life. Its impending collapse signifies the fragility and vulnerability of the frameworks – be they physical or spiritual – that uphold us. Through fixing the wall, Al Khidr guarantees that the concealed treasure beneath it stays safeguarded until its owners, two orphaned boys, reach maturity and can rightfully inherit it.

Repairing the wall without seeking anything in exchange showcases the idea of kindness. It emphasizes the significance of upkeeping and safeguarding what holds value and importance even when met with ungratefulness or animosity. The wall symbolizes the facets of knowledge that work to shield and uphold life, often without acknowledgment or recompense.

The Revelation of the Hidden Treasure:

Al Khidr eventually reveals that beneath the wall lies a treasure belonging to the orphans. This treasure symbolizes blessings and presents protected by fate often unbeknownst to us. Repairing the wall ensures that the treasure remains concealed and safeguarded until the boys reach an age where they can benefit from it.

The story highlights the idea of insight and protection. It shows how actions of safeguarding and support, when they appear small or senseless at first, ultimately contribute to a plan, in line with divine fairness and kindness.

The Balance of Creation and Destruction:

The rebuilding of the wall stands in contrast to the instances of damage (the smashing of the boat) and aggression (the slaying of the boy). The interplay between building and tearing down serves as a motif throughout the journey.

Chapter 7

The Unveiling of Wisdom:

At the end of their adventure, Al Khidr discloses the underlying motives behind his puzzling behaviours. This section plays a role in grasping the knowledge that shapes the world, emphasizing how human understanding is restricted and the importance of having faith in divine direction. The revelation of wisdom becomes a moment of realization, for Moses showcasing how patience, modesty and belief can bring about change.

The Moment of Revelation:

After completing the task of repairing the wall, Moses is again puzzled by Al Khidr's behaviour. It is at this juncture that Al Khidr chooses to unveil the meaning behind all their shared experiences. This moment of enlightenment serves not to explain actions, but instead to impart a profound teaching, on comprehending divine wisdom and human existence.

Al Khidr's insights offer Moses a view showing how every deed, even if it appears unfair or illogical at first glance, has a greater significance. This unveiling acts as a symbol of the growth that accompanies perseverance and modesty, uncovering the realities concealed within our life encounters.

The Significance of Each Act:

1. The Breaking of the Boat:

Al Khidr shared that he damaged the boat to prevent it from being seized by a king who was confiscating all ships. The harm inflicted on the boat at first ended up preventing a catastrophe for its owners, ensuring their livelihood was protected. This story teaches us that making sacrifices in the short term can result in long term advantages.

2. The Killing of the Boy:

Al Khidr shares that the young boy had a fate of becoming someone who would bring pain and hardship to his loved ones and society. Through his intervention, Al Khidr averted this calamity, shielding many from anguish. This action highlights the idea that divine justice sometimes demands choices that surpass comprehension, underlining the importance of having faith in a greater purpose.

3. The Restoration of the Wall:

The wall held a stash intended for two boys who had lost their parents left behind by their caring father. Al Khidr's actions, in fixing the wall, ensured that the treasure would stay safe and out of sight until the boys were mature enough to discover it. This gesture exemplifies the idea of protection and planning, illustrating how efforts to safeguard something can lead to positive outcomes in the long run.

The Nature of Divine Wisdom:

Al Khidr's wisdom offers perspectives on facets of understanding:

1. Holistic Perspective:

In the realm of insight, a comprehensive perspective on life is embraced, taking into consideration the reaching and interrelated effects of decisions. In contrast, to comprehension, which tends to focus on tangible results divine wisdom acknowledges the overarching and hidden ramifications.

2. Protective and Preventive Measures:

Al Khidr often takes actions to safeguard people and communities from significant harm. This aspect of wisdom underscores the value of faith during difficult times, acknowledging that what seems detrimental now could actually be a form of long term protection.

3. Compassion and Justice:

Compassion and justice intertwine as themes in the narrative. The wisdom of the divine is guided by compassion, even if its decisions may appear severe or unfair, to us. This harmony guarantees that fairness prevails in a manner that ultimately serves the welfare of humanity.

4. Patience and Humility:

The journey highlights the significance of being patient and humble, in the quest for knowledge. Moses's initial impatience and quick judgments are juxtaposed with the insights gained through Al Khidr's explanations. This teaching promotes embracing a patient attitude towards life's obstacles, having faith in the revelation of wisdom.

The Transformative Power of Revelation:

The revelation of wisdom profoundly affects Moses's life, enhancing his awareness of the constraints of perception and the importance of believing in direction. This change plays a role in his development, demonstrating how instances of insight can trigger significant shifts in how one views and navigates life.

The tale of Moses and Al Khidr symbolizes the essence of being human, emphasizing the significance of delving into comprehension, practising patience and humility, and having faith in a wisdom that navigates the world. This metamorphosis transcends intellectuality; it delves into spirituality, fostering a more harmonious outlook on existence.

Lessons for Contemporary Life:

Moses's enlightening journey, with Al Khidr, offers insights for life:

1. Embrace Uncertainty:

Life is brimming with surprises that throw obstacles our way without a clear explanation. This story encourages individuals to embrace ambiguity, with serenity and trust, recognizing that significant discoveries may reveal themselves as time unfolds.

2. Trust in the Process:

Embarking on this path highlights the significance of having faith, in the journey of education and personal development. In times of challenges or perceived unfairness, it's crucial to believe in a design that offers a view of things.

3. Seek Deeper Understanding:

The story promotes a search for comprehension, delving beneath the surface to reveal the profound insights hidden within life's happenings. This pursuit includes challenging assumptions, embracing intricacies, and staying receptive to perspectives.

4. Balance Justice and Compassion:

This story highlights the value of balance, fairness and compassion. Additionally, it also speaks of the requirement of incorporating aforementioned values into our daily choices and attitudes. This reassures us that justice is hand in hand with empathy and understanding.

The Broader Implications:

Moses's adventure, with Al Khidr, sheds light on meanings about guidance and human nature. It shows how everything is connected, and even small actions can lead to outcomes that may not be obvious at first glance.

The story also highlights how moments of realization and understanding can bring about shifts in one's outlook and attitude towards life, nurturing a sense of empathy, modesty and faith.

Conclusion:

The story of Moses and Al Khidr reveals wisdom about guidance, human perception limits, and the importance of patience, humility and faith. Let's draw inspiration from their journey to face life's uncertainties, with trust and patience. May we seek wisdom in our paths as we navigate through life's twists and turns.

Chapter 8

Lessons from the Journey:

The tale of Moses and Al Khidr is brimming with teachings that hold significance throughout history and different societies. It provides insights into wisdom, patience, humility and spirituality. This section summarizes the lessons learned from their expedition, focusing on faith, comprehension and personal growth. By exploring these teachings, we can gain an understanding of the enduring wisdom woven into their narrative. Use these reflections to enrich our own experiences.

The Importance of Patience:

The concept of patience plays a role in the story of Moses and Al Khidr. Right from the start, Al Khidr stresses the need for Moses to maintain patience and avoid questioning his decisions until the reasons behind them are made clear. This insistence underscores the value of tolerating ambiguity and having faith in the learning journey.

1. Enduring Uncertainty:

It's important to remain patient when dealing with uncertainty and confusion. Moses' impatience at first, followed by his comprehension, highlights the importance of waiting for all the information before forming opinions. This message holds true in today's fast-paced society, where there's a push to seek quick fixes and responses.

2. The Process of Learning:

Real knowledge and comprehension require patience. The path underscores that wisdom isn't gained overnight. Through a journey of learning and contemplation, being patient enables us to grasp and incorporate perspectives profoundly.

3. Cultivating Inner Peace:

Having patience is essential for discovering peace. Recognizing that some solutions may require time to emerge reduces anxiety and nurtures a sense of calm during periods.

The Value of Humility:

Learning about humility is a takeaway from the journey. Moses, a prophet, shows humility by seeking out Al Khidr and recognizing his own thirst for more knowledge. This humble approach is vital for gaining wisdom, as it allows for embracing viewpoints and delving into deeper insights.

1. Acknowledging Limitations:

Understanding our boundaries is a great move towards progress. Moses's openness to gaining knowledge from Al Khidr, despite his position, illustrates the significance of modesty in seeking wisdom. It serves as a reminder that regardless of our accomplishments, there is always room for learning.

2. Openness to Guidance:

Having humility means being willing to accept advice from others. The importance of seeking wisdom from individuals with knowledge and experience is highlighted by Al Khidr's role, as a mentor. This receptiveness encourages learning and development.

3. Fostering Respectful Relationships:

Acknowledging and appreciating the skills and knowledge of others helps create an environment of respect and collaboration, fostering a space for building relationships and supporting development.

Trust in Divine Wisdom:

One important part of the journey involves having faith in wisdom. When Moses accompanies Al Khidr, he must trust in a power, when Al Khidr's actions seem puzzling, as they are believed to be guided by a greater wisdom.

1. Faith Beyond Understanding:

Having faith in wisdom means believing when we can't grasp the reasons behind things. Al Khidr's justifications show that his actions, though appearing tough, are for a purpose. This teaching urges us to have confidence in the plan during challenging and uncertain times.

2. Surrendering Control:

Trusting in the wisdom of the plan entails letting go of the urge to control and fully grasp everything. This act of surrender is not about giving up, it's about embracing faith, acknowledging that certain truths are beyond our human understanding.

3. Finding Meaning in Adversity:

The voyage shows us that facing challenges can lead to insights and growth. By having faith in guidance, we can discover lessons and progress in situations, knowing that they play a role in shaping our spiritual and personal journey.

The Role of Compassion and Justice:

Compassion and justice play a role in Al Khidr's decisions. Despite appearing strict at first, his actions are actually driven by compassion and a long term view, safeguarding people from harm and upholding justice.

1. Complexity of Justice:

The tale shows that justice is intricate and has facets. Al Khidr's deeds, though first seen as unfair, turn out to be acts of justice that avert further pain. This intricacy questions ideas of good and bad, promoting an understanding of justice.

2. Compassionate Action:

Genuine empathy sometimes involves making choices that take into account how they will affect people and communities in the long run. Al Khidr's decisions are driven by a sense of caring for people's well-being, underscoring the significance of reflecting on the wider consequences of our choices.

3. Balancing Compassion and Justice:

Balancing compassion and justice is essential when making decisions. Al Khidr's deeds showcase this equilibrium, demonstrating that genuine wisdom combines both values to benefit the good.

The Transformative Power of Knowledge:

The tale of Moses and Al Khidr illustrates the power of knowledge to ignite change. As Moses explores viewpoints, he acquires wisdom and his spiritual quest blossoms.

1. Knowledge as Transformation:

Genuine understanding has the ability to change how we see things and the way we behave. The experience shows that true wisdom isn't about gathering information. It is a journey that alters how we perceive the world.

2. Continuous Growth:

Continuous learning is a never-ending journey, as illustrated by Moses's story highlighting the importance of staying open to experiences and insights, throughout life.

3. Integration of Knowledge:

Integrating knowledge into our experiences is crucial for gaining genuine wisdom. Moses's contemplation of Al Khidr's deeds highlights the significance of comprehending and utilizing insights, for spiritual development.

Practical Applications of the Lessons:

The teachings derived from the adventures of Moses and Al Khidr hold relevance in all times, providing insights, for growth and spiritual enrichment:

1. Practising Patience:

Embracing patience in our routines can assist us in managing unpredictability and obstacles smoothly. Recognizing that certain solutions require time enables us to handle circumstances with composure and strength.

2. Embracing Humility:

Recognizing and accepting humility allows us to remain open to learning and growth. Appreciating viewpoints and understanding our boundaries fosters a spirit of teamwork and mutual respect in the quest for knowledge.

3. Trusting the Process:

Having faith in the journey of life and drawing motivation from sources can guide us towards discovering significance in certain times. Letting go of control and embracing belief empowers us to confront challenges, with positivity and confidence.

4. Balancing Compassion and Justice:

Finding a blend of kindness and fairness in our behaviour can greatly impact those around us. Striking this equilibrium is crucial in decision making and nurturing connections with others.

5. Continuous Learning:

Embracing learning and personal development enables us to stay flexible and receptive to ideas. Through exploration for insights we gain the ability to navigate life's intricacies with knowledge and perspective.

Conclusion:

The story of Moses and Al Khidr's adventure imparts lessons on qualities such as patience, humility and trust in guidance. It underscores the importance of pursuing truth and confronting life's challenges with belief and a receptive attitude.

Looking back on their journey, let's use their experiences as motivation to develop these characteristics in our lives. By being patient, staying humble, having faith in the process, finding a balance between compassion and justice, and staying committed to learning, we can navigate our journeys with more wisdom and insight.

The tale of Moses and Al Khidr illustrates the notion that genuine wisdom involves evolution and development. It encourages us to immerse ourselves in our experiences, have faith in the unfolding of wisdom, and stay receptive to the opportunities for learning and personal development. Their narrative serves as a reminder that seeking wisdom's not merely an objective, but a continuous voyage that enhances our existence and broadens our insight into both the world around us and our inner selves.

Chapter 9

The Path of the Seeker:

Moses's journey with Al Khidr symbolizes the timeless pursuit of knowledge and insight. It underscores the virtues needed by those in search of wisdom, stressing the significance of determination, inquisitiveness, modesty and openness to ambiguity. This section explores the characteristics that distinguish a seeker and considers how Moses and Al Khidr's narrative can motivate and steer individuals on their paths of spiritual growth.

The Essence of Seeking:

Exploring is a part of being human fuelled by a sense of curiosity and a longing to unravel life's mysteries. For Moses this search isn't about intellect, but about a spiritual exploration. His choice to find Al Khidr shows that genuine wisdom can be found beyond what's known and may need the help of those with profound insight.

Delving into the core of seeking entails embarking on a quest of self-exploration and personal development. It necessitates being open to experiences and having a thirst for knowledge and broadening one's perspective. This journey of discovery is not a route but an ongoing cycle that encompasses moments of uncertainty, enlightenment and change.

Qualities of a True Seeker:

1. Perseverance:

The path of a soul is often marked by obstacles and hardships. It's essential to possess resolve to conquer these obstacles and remain committed to the quest for wisdom. The tale of Moses journeying alongside Al Khidr underscores the significance of persistence, in confronting trials and uncertainties, trusting that each challenge contributes to enlightenment.

2. Curiosity:

A genuine seeker is motivated by a curiosity and a longing to unveil the realities of life. This inquisitiveness propels the quest for wisdom, and promotes venturing into territories. Moses's readiness to embark on an expedition with Al Khidr, despite the obstacles, illustrates the significance of upholding a receptive attitude towards learning.

3. Humility:

Having humility is essential for individuals who are on a quest for wisdom. It means acknowledging the boundaries of one's knowledge and being willing to gain insights from others. The encounters between Moses and Al Khidr underscore the importance of humility, in the journey of acquiring knowledge, as Moses is consistently advised to have faith and learn from his mentor.

4. Embracing Uncertainty:

The quest for knowledge often requires navigating through doubt and vagueness. A sincere seeker must be ready to welcome the unfamiliar and stay receptive to discovering insights in many ways. Moses's expedition, with Al Khidr, highlights the significance of accepting ambiguity as each challenge uncovers profound levels of comprehension that were previously concealed.

5. Openness to Transformation:

The journey of a seeker is one marked by growth and evolution. A genuine seeker remains receptive to the changes brought about by their experiences and revelations, enabling them to develop and enhance their comprehension. Moses's encounter with Al Khidr exemplifies the impact of seeking as he acquires insights that alter his perspective on divine wisdom.

The Journey of Moses and Al Khidr:

The story of Moses travelling with Al Khidr symbolizes a search for wisdom. Every challenge and meeting they experience teaches lessons about the essence of knowledge and the characteristics needed to seek it.

1. The Breaking of the Boat:

This occasion underscores the value of maintaining composure and optimism in all times, prompting people to explore and grasp the importance of circumstances.

2. The Killing of the Boy:

This emphasizes the importance of embodying the complexities and the unknown behind knowledge. It is a lesson, that real understanding, more often than not, involves confronting realities.

3. The Restoration of the Wall:

This occasion underscores the significance of empathy. Being prepared in advance, stressing the importance of safeguarding, and treasuring what matters. It promotes responding with compassion and consideration, in scenarios marked by ungratefulness or hostility.

4. The Unveiling of Wisdom:

The realization, at the conclusion of the adventure, serves as a reminder of how human perception has its boundaries and the importance of having faith in direction. It instils in the explorer a belief in the unveiling of wisdom, acknowledging that profound truths are frequently hidden beneath surface comprehension.

Applying the Lessons to Contemporary Life:

The story of Moses and Al Khidr offers insights for individuals seeking guidance through life's challenges:

1. Maintain Perseverance in the Face of Challenges:

Life is full of challenges and unknowns. The narrative motivates people to keep pushing in their quest for wisdom and insight, believing that every encounter adds to their development.

2. Cultivate Curiosity and Openness:

Approaching life with a sense of curiosity and openness encourages learning and discovery. By embracing wonder and inquisitiveness, people can reveal insights; thus, broadening their knowledge.

3. Practise Humility and Receptiveness:

Understanding one's limitations and being receptive to learning from others are aspects of humility. It plays a role in the pursuit of wisdom, enabling development and personal transformation.

4. Embrace Uncertainty and Complexity:

Life is filled with many plot twists. The story reminds us to fulfil these complexities of life with faith, with the realization that clarity will eventually come.

5. Be Open to Transformation:

Embarking on a quest for knowledge is a process that leads to growth and transformation. By embracing the changes brought about by life experiences, people can expand their insights and progress, along their journey.

The Broader Implications:

The journey of those seeking holds meaning, in grasping existence and the essence of insight. It emphasizes how all encounters are linked, and the significance of embracing an inquisitive attitude towards life. The quest for knowledge goes beyond exploration; it delves into a profoundly spiritual quest, for ongoing development and change.

This story also stresses the value of being guided, persevering and having humility. Whenever in the pursuit of knowledge, it's important for individuals to realize the limits of their knowledge.

Conclusion:

The seeker's journey, as seen in the tales of Moses and Al Khidr, is a moving experience that resonates with the essence of being human. It underscores the values and mindsets for seeking wisdom, emphasizing the significance of determination, inquisitiveness, modesty, and openness to ambiguity. While we tread our paths, let us find motivation in this narrative, embracing the impact of exploration and having faith, in the revelation of spiritual insight.

Chapter 10

Beyond the Unseen Path:

The story of Moses and Al Khidr, while unique, the journey touches upon timeless themes that go beyond any era or society. In this concluding section, we delve into the meanings of their adventure, pondering the essence of wisdom and how it shapes our experiences. Through drawing lessons from their encounters, we uncover perspectives on the never-ending pursuit of knowledge, the interdependence among all living beings, and the eternal quest for insight that propels humanity forward.

The Continuous Journey of Seeking:

The tale of Moses and Al Khidr showcases how the quest for wisdom is a voyage. It doesn't reach a pinnacle in one moment of enlightenment. It entails discovery, education and change. This perspective questions the idea of wisdom as a fixed destination, suggesting instead that it's a journey that develops with every encounter and realization.

1. The Evolution of Understanding:

Moses's experiences with Al Khidr show how each event and revelation adds to the next, leading to a detailed grasp of wisdom. This progression mirrors how humans learn, gaining insights from a combination of experiences.

2. Perpetual Curiosity:

The story emphasizes the importance of maintaining a sense of curiosity and openness throughout life. This perpetual curiosity drives the continuous search for deeper truths and fosters an attitude of humility and receptiveness.

3. Adaptability and Growth:

Embarking on a quest demands flexibility and a readiness to evolve. When we uncover perspectives, it's crucial to be open, to reevaluate our convictions and fine-tune our comprehension. This ability to adapt is vital for one's spiritual development.

The Interconnectedness of All Beings:

The tale of Moses and Al Khidr shows how everything and everyone is linked. Even small deeds can lead to repercussions that go way beyond our initial understanding.

1. *The Ripple Effect:*

Al Khidr's deeds, such as damaging the boat or repairing the wall, demonstrate the effects of actions. This idea promotes a perspective on life, acknowledging that each choice plays a part in the tapestry of existence.

2. *Collective Responsibility:*

The concept that there is an interconnectedness among all living beings suggests that we have a duty to look out for each other. This narrative illustrates that demonstrating acts of compassion, understanding and justice is not an endeavour but brings advantages to society and the global community.

3. *Empathy and Compassion:*

Recognizing the interconnectedness of all living creatures nurtures empathy and kindness. When we acknowledge how our actions affect everyone around us, it inspires us to approach life with thoughtfulness and compassion for others.

The Ultimate Quest for Understanding:

The tale of Moses and Al Khidr symbolizes the timeless pursuit for knowledge, delving into not facts but also spiritual and existential wisdom. This journey stems from a yearning to grasp the enigmas of existence and the celestial laws guiding our world.

1. The Limits of Human Perception:

The story highlights how people's understanding has limits and the importance of having faith in wisdom. It questions the arrogance of thinking we can comprehend all truths through logic, promoting a harmony between exploration and belief.

2. The Role of Faith and Trust:

In the pursuit of knowledge, belief and reliance hold importance. Moses's expedition exemplifies how genuine insight frequently demands a step into the unknown, placing faith in what's unseen. This confidence isn't naive but grounded in an acknowledgment of our boundaries and the immense depth of understanding.

3. Embracing Mystery and Wonder:

Delving into the depths of knowledge entails embracing the enigmas and marvels of our existence. It necessitates a readiness to acknowledge the uncertainties and an openness to grapple with the intricacies of life without expecting solutions.

Practical Applications for Contemporary Life:

The deeper meanings behind the tale of Moses and Al Khidr provide insights for dealing with modern day challenges.

1. Lifelong Learning:

The ongoing quest for knowledge highlights the significance of education. In a world that is constantly evolving, embracing curiosity and staying receptive to concepts are crucial for individual and career development.

2. Holistic Perspective:

The interconnectedness among all living beings promotes an approach to making decisions. When we take into account the effects of our choices, we can opt for actions that benefit not ourselves but also others and the natural world.

3. Balancing Reason and Faith:

The journey towards comprehension emphasizes the importance of blending exploration with belief and confidence. This equilibrium promotes a method for addressing challenges and self-improvement, merging reasoning with inner spiritual wisdom.

4. Embracing Uncertainty:

Life is inherently uncertain, and the story encourages individuals to embrace this uncertainty with courage and resilience. By accepting the unknown, we can navigate challenges with greater flexibility and adaptability.

Reflections on Divine Wisdom:

The tale of Moses and Al Khidr offers insights into the essence of wisdom and how it influences our experiences.

1. Unseen Guidance:

The wisdom of the divine is often at work through guidance shaping outcomes and choices in ways that may not be obvious at first. Trusting in the scheme of things and acknowledging our limited knowledge is key to following this guidance.

2. Compassionate Justice:

Compassion and justice intertwine as elements in the narrative. The tale emphasizes the importance of harmonizing insight to guide actions that benefit society as a whole, all while upholding empathy and consideration for each person's well-being.

3. Transformative Power:

The profound wisdom bestowed upon us has the ability to reshape how we perceive and navigate through life. When we embrace this wisdom, we open ourselves up to spiritual development, allowing us to gain a deeper understanding of the essence of our existence.

Conclusion:

The tale of Moses and Al Khidr teaches us enduring lessons, on the never-ending search for knowledge, unity among all living things and the relentless pursuit of enlightenment.

When we look back on their tale it brings to mind the value of learning, seeing the bigger picture, finding a balance between logic and belief, and embracing ambiguity. These core beliefs help us navigate the complexities of life, nurturing our spiritual development. Along this journey we learn to recognize the wisdom that shapes the world, urging us to have faith in what's hidden and unknown, and to approach all our pursuits with kindness and fairness. As we follow our journeys, we may find motivation in the story of Moses and Al Khidr, embracing the strength of exploration and uncovering deeper truths, beyond what is visible.

Overall Conclusion: The Eternal Quest for Divine Wisdom:

The story of Moses and Al Khidr, in "Demystify, The Unseen Path" symbolizes the quest for wisdom, understanding and spiritual enlightenment in humankind. Their story transcends boundaries, offering timeless lessons that resonate with seekers of truth throughout history. This comprehensive examination weaves together the teachings and insights gained from their journey, reflecting on the impact of knowledge, the importance of humility and faith, and the enduring significance of their tale, in life.

The Transformative Power of Divine Wisdom:

The interactions between Moses and Al Khidr showcase how divine wisdom can bring about transformations, working in ways that surpass understanding. Through each challenge and revelation they face on their journey, Moses's beliefs grow in value. His perception of the plan grows.

1. Layers of Understanding:

The deep essence of wisdom urges people to explore beyond superficial understandings to reveal valuable insights. The initial feelings that Moses goes through upon witnessing Al Khidr's actions – confusion, anger and disbelief – mirror the struggles we face when dealing with life's complexities. This journey highlights that wisdom is not a possession but a continuous process of gaining and letting go of knowledge.

2. Beyond Conventional Morality:

The story questions ideas of what's right and wrong, highlighting how divine fairness and kindness can go beyond human ideas of morality. Al Khidr's behaviour, though puzzling, shows an intention connected to a kinder view of justice. This perspective promotes an understanding way of dealing with moral conflicts in our daily lives.

3. Personal and Spiritual Growth:

The adventure changes not only Moses but everyone involved in their tale. It highlights the chance for spiritual development that comes from accepting the unknown and having faith in the plan. When we think about what they've been through, it prompts us to go through our own changes, gaining wisdom and understanding.

The Importance of Humility and Trust:

The core of Moses and Al Khidr's journey revolves around the importance of humility and trust. These attributes play a role for individuals embarking on a quest, as they allow for a profound insight and spiritual direction.

1. Humility in Learning:

Moses's decision to approach Al Khidr and admit his shortcomings demonstrates the humility needed for learning. This humility isn't about putting oneself down. Rather, about acknowledging the vastness of wisdom and the constraints of human understanding.

2. Trust in the Unseen:

Moses demonstrated patience by refraining from questioning, emphasizing the significance of having faith in the wisdom of plans. This level of trust surpasses logic, embracing life's facets with confidence that every event occurs for a purpose.

3. Openness to Guidance:

The narrative underscores the significance of embracing advice from individuals, with insight. Al Khidr's function as a mentor underscores the importance of guidance. The wisdom gained from those who have journeyed ahead of us. This receptiveness encourages a generational attitude, towards pursuing knowledge.

Enduring Relevance to Contemporary Life:

The tale of Moses and Al Khidr holds enduring wisdom to the intricacies and dilemmas of modern day living. In a shifting world filled with uncertainties and ethical grey areas, their experiences offer lessons for both individual development and societal progress.

1. Navigating Uncertainty:

In an era of constant change and unpredictability, the ability to navigate uncertainty with patience and trust is crucial. The story encourages us to embrace uncertainty as an integral part of the human experience, fostering resilience and adaptability.

2. Holistic Perspective:

The way everything and everyone are connected, as shown through Al Khidr's deeds, promotes an approach to decision making. This viewpoint is crucial for tackling issues, like protecting the environment, promoting fairness and addressing economic disparities, while acknowledging that what we do can have widespread consequences.

3. Ethical Complexity:

The story urges us to look past assessments and delve into the ethical intricacies of existence. When we take into account the scope and lasting effects of our choices, we can arrive at more empathetic conclusions.

4. Lifelong Learning:

The ongoing quest for knowledge highlights the significance of learning and progress. In a changing society, embracing curiosity, receptiveness and modesty is crucial for career advancement.

Reflecting on the Journey:

The journey of Moses and Al Khidr is a profound metaphor for the human quest for meaning and understanding. It invites us to reflect on our own paths, recognizing the trials and revelations that shape our experiences and contribute to our growth.

1. Embracing the Unknown:

The tale prompts us to welcome the unfamiliar and the enigmas of life, with bravery and belief. By releasing the desire for solutions and having faith in the revelation of insight, we can manoeuvre through life's obstacles with more comfort and poise.

2. Balancing Reason and Faith:

The story focuses on finding harmony between logic and belief, emphasizing the importance of blending thinking with wisdom for a well-rounded perspective on life.

3. Acting with Compassion and Justice:

The values of empathy and fairness that form the basis of Al Khidr's deeds can inspire us to behave in a positive manner. When we show kindness and take responsibility for the welfare of others, we play a part in shaping a fairer society.

Conclusion:

The tale of Moses and Al Khidr as observed in "Demystify: The Unseen Path" delves into revelations about the essence of knowledge, the significance of being humble and having faith, and the ongoing pursuit for insight that characterizes human life. Their narrative serves as a timeless lesson on the impact of exploration, urging us to approach life's enigmas with bravery, inquisitiveness and empathy.

Looking back on the path they've travelled can motivate us to approach our journeys with patience and humility, believing in the reveal of wisdom. It's important to recognize the interconnectedness of all beings and ponder the reaching effects of our choices. Remain receptive to the wisdom and revelations that emerge from our encounters, allowing them to mould and enrich our existence.

The pursuit of wisdom is a voyage that encourages us to delve into the depths of our comprehension and the infinite wonders of the cosmos. The tale of Moses and Al Khidr serves as a reminder that this expedition is not just achievable but also deeply rewarding, presenting limitless chances for development, change and illumination.

CURRICULUM VITAE
PROFESSOR DR. KAMIL IDRIS

Former Director General
(elected by the Coordination Committee and the General Assembly)
World Intellectual Property Organization
(WIPO), United Nations Specialised Agency

Former Secretary-General
(elected by the Council)
International Union for the Protection of New Varieties
of Plants (UPOV)

Former Member (elected by the United Nations General Assembly)
United Nations International Law
Commission (ILC)
Former Ambassador

Former President
World Arbitration and Mediation Court (WAMC)

Member
Permanent Court of Arbitration (PCA),The Hague

President
The International Court of Arbitration and Mediation (ICAM)

ACADEMIC DISTINCTIONS

LLB (Law), University of Khartoum (Honors)

Bachelor of Arts, Philosophical Studies, University of Cairo (Honors)

Diploma, Public Administration (Management Department), Institute of Public Administration, Khartoum

Master in International Affairs (MAIA), University of Ohio, USA (First Class Average)

Doctorate (PhD) in International Law, Graduate Institute of International Studies, University of Geneva (Distinction)

Doctorate Thesis: "Case study on the Treaty Establishing a Preferential Trade Area for Eastern and Southern African States"

ACADEMIC INTERESTS
Certificates
International Economics, Graduate Institute of International Studies (Geneva)

International History and Political Science, Graduate Institute of International Studies (Geneva)

International Law of Development, Graduate Institute of International Studies (Geneva)

The Law of International Waterways, Graduate Institute of International Studies (Geneva)

International Law of Financing and Banking Systems, Graduate Institute of International Studies (Geneva)

Languages
Arabic, English, French, Spanish (good knowledge)

Teaching
Lecturer in Philosophy and Jurisprudence,
University of Cairo (1976-1977)

Lecturer in Jurisprudence, Ohio University, USA (1978)

External Examiner in International Law, Faculty of Law, University of Khartoum (1984)

Lecturer in Intellectual Property Law, Faculty of Law, University of Khartoum (1986)

Lecturer in several international, regional and national seminars, workshops and symposia

Member, International Association for the
Advancement of Teaching and Research in
Intellectual Property Law (ATRIP)

Decorations

Awarded the Scholars and Researchers State Gold
Medal, presented by the President of the Republic
of the Sudan (1983)

Awarded the Scholars and Researchers Gold Medal,
presented by the President of the Academy of
Scientific Research and Technology of Egypt (1985)

Awarded the decoration of the Commandeur de
l'Ordre national du Lion, Senegal (1998)

Awarded the Medal of the Bolshoi Theatre, presented
by the Director of the Bolshoi Theatre, Russian
Federation (1999)

Awarded the Honorary Medal, presented by the Rector
of the Moscow State Institute of International
Relations, Russian Federation (1999)

Awarded the Honorary Medal of The Gulf Cooperation
Council (GCC), Saudi Arabia (1999)

Awarded the Golden Plaque of the Town of Banská
Bystrica, presented by the Mayor of Banská
Bystrica, Slovakia (1999)

Awarded the Golden Medal of Matej Bel University,
presented by the Dean of the University, Banská
Bystrica, Slovakia (1999)

Awarded the Silver Jubilee Medal of the Eurasian
Patent Organization (EAPO), presented by Mr.
Viktor Blinnikov, President of the Eurasian Patent
Office, Russian Federation (2000)

Award of Distinguished Merit, presented by the
Egyptian Supreme Council for Science and
Technology, Egypt (2000)

Awarded a Plaque from the Syrian Inventors'
Association, Syrian Arab Republic (2000)

Awarded the Grand Cross of the Infante D. Enrique,
Portugal (2001)

Awarded a Medal from the People's Assembly of Egypt,
Egypt (2001)

Awarded a Medal from the Constitutional Court of
Romania, Romania (2001)

Awarded a Medal from the Parliament of Romania,
Romania (2001)

Awarded the Golden Medal Dolores del Río al Mérito
internacional en favor de los derechos de los
artistas intérpretes from the National Association
of Interpreters (ANDI), Mexico (2001)

Awarded the Golden Medal from The State Agency on
Industrial Property Protection, Republic of Moldova
(2001)

Awarded the decoration of the Commandeur de l'Ordre
du Mérite national, Côte d'Ivoire (2002)

Awarded the Maria Sklodowska-Curie Medal from the Association of Polish Inventors and Rationalizers, Poland (2002)

Awarded the decoration of The Order of the Two Niles, First Class, from the President of the Republic of Sudan, Sudan (2002)

Kamil Idris Library, University of Juba, Sudan (2002)

Kamil Idris Conference Hall, Intellectual Property Court, The Judiciary, Sudan (2002)

Awarded the Dank Medal (medal of glory), from the President of the Kyrgyz Republic, Kyrgyzstan (2003)

Award from the University of National and World Economy, Bulgaria (2003)

"Venice Award for Intellectual Property", presented by the Mayor of Venice (2004)

Awarded the Medal of Oman, presented by His Royal Highness Fahid Bin Mahmud Al-Said, Deputy Prime Minister of the Council of Ministers, Oman (2004)

Awarded the decoration of the Aztec Eagle, presented by Ambassador Luis Alfonso de Alba (Permanent Representative of Mexico to International Organizations in Geneva) on behalf of Presidente of Mexico Vicente Fox, (2005)

Kamil Idris Building, Regional Training Center, African Regional Intellectual Property Organization (ARIPO), Harare, Zimbabwe (2006)

Awarded a Medal commemorating the 60 years of the United Nations, Bulgaria (2006)

Awarded a Medal commemorating the 60 years of the Independence of Jordan, Jordan (2006)

Award of Distinguished Leadership presented by the International Publishers' Association (IPA) and the Arab Publishers Association, Egypt (2007)

Awarded a Medal on the occasion of the Fujairah International Monodrama Festival, Fujairah, United Arab Emirates (2007)

Awarded a Medal on the occasion of the Intellectual Property Day presented by The Regional Institute for Intellectual Property of the Faculty of Law, University of Helwan, Egypt (2008)

Awarded The Distinguished Medal of Cultural Innovation, Sudan (2008)

Awarded The Family Club Decoration, Sudan (2008)

Awarded The World Intellectual Property Organization (WIPO) Medal, Geneva, Switzerland(2008)

Awarded The International Union Of The Protection Of New Varieties Of Plants (UPOV)

Medal, Geneva, Switzerland (2008)

Awarded The Distinguished Medal Of The Sudanese Centre Of Intellectual Property, Khartoum, Sudan (2009)

Awarded The Medal Of Kenana sugar Company, Khartoum , Sudan (2009)

Awarded The Decoration Of Loyalty And Gratitude Of Omdurman National Broadcasting Station, Sudan (2010)

Awarded The decoration (WISHAH) of the Syrian revolution (2013)

Awarded The decoration (WISHAH) of Rashid Diab cultural center, Khartoum , Sudan (2013)

Awarded The Medal of Distinction by the International Association of Muslim

Lawyers (2014)

Honorary Degrees

1999 Honorary Professor of Law, Peking University, China

1999 Doctor Honoris Causa, The Doctor's Council of the State University of Moldova, Republic of Moldova

1999 Doctor Honoris Causa, Franklin Pierce Law Center (Concord, New Hampshire), United States of America

1999 Doctor Honoris Causa, Fudan University (Shanghai), China

2000 Doctor Honoris Causa, University of National and World Economy (Sofia), Bulgaria

2001 Doctor Honoris Causa, University of Bucharest, Romania

2001 Doctor Honoris Causa, Hannam University (Daejeon), Republic of Korea

2001 Doctor Honoris Causa, Mongolian University of Science and Technology (Ulaanbaatar), Mongolia

2001 Doctor Honoris Causa, Matej Bel University (Banská Bystrica), Slovakia

2002 Doctor Honoris Causa, National Technical University of Ukraine "Kyiv Polytechnic Institute" (Kyiv), Ukraine

2003 Doctor Honoris Causa, Al Eman Al Mahdi University (White Nile State), Sudan

2005 Degree of Doctor of Letters (Honoris Causa), Indira Gandhi National Open University (IGNOU), India

2005 Doctor Honoris Causa, Latvian Academy of Sciences, Latvia

2006 Doctor Honoris Causa, University of Azerbaijan, Azerbaijan

2007 Doctor Honoris Causa, University of Al-Gezira, Sudan

2007 Doctor of International Law and Honorary Professor, Belarussian State University, Belarus

2007 Doctor Honoris Causa, University of Khartoum, Sudan

2007 Doctor Honoris Causa, Ss. Cyril and Methodius University (Skopje), The Former Yugoslav Republic of Macedonia

2008 Doctor Honoris Causa, Kyrgyz State University of Construction, Transport and Architecture (Bishkek), Kyrgystan

2008 Certificate of Appreciation, Ahlia University, Khartoum, Sudan

2020 Honorary Professor, Durham University (United Kingdom)

EXPERIENCE
Professional

Part-time Journalist, El-Ayam and El-Sahafa (Sudanese) newspapers (1971-1979)

Lecturer, University of Cairo (1976)

Assistant Director, Arab Department, Ministry of Foreign Affairs, Khartoum (1977)

Assistant Director, Research Department, Ministry of Foreign Affairs, Khartoum (January-June 1978)

Deputy Director, Legal Department, Ministry of Foreign Affairs, Khartoum (July-December 1978)

Member of Sudan Permanent Mission to the United Nations Office, Geneva (1979-1982)

Vice-Consul of Sudan in Switzerland (1979-1982)

Legal Adviser of Sudan Permanent Mission to the United Nations Office, Geneva (1979-1982)

Senior Program Officer, Development Cooperation and External Relations Bureau for Africa, World

Intellectual Property Organization (WIPO), (1982-1985)

Director, Development Cooperation and External Relations Bureau for Arab and Central and Eastern European Countries, WIPO (1985-1994)

Ambassador, Ministry of Foreign Affairs, Sudan (current status at national level)

Deputy Director General, WIPO (1994-1997)

Director General, WIPO, since 1997

Secretary-General, International Union for the Protection of Plant Varieties (UPOV), since 1997

Special

External Assessor for the title of Professor, College of Islamic Studies (CIS), Sheikh Hamad University, Doha, Qatar 2024

Member of The Academic Council, University of Khartoum (Sudan, April 2007)

Member, Board of Trustees, Nile Valley University (Egypt, June 2000)

Member, United Nations International Law Commission (ILC) (2000-2001)

Member, Advisory Council on Intellectual Property (ACIP), Franklin Pierce Law Center (Concord, New Hampshire, 1999)

Member, United Nations International Law Commission (ILC) (1992-1996)

Vice-Chairman of the International Law Commission (ILC) at its 45th session (1993)

Representative of the ILC in the 35th session of the Asian-African Legal Consultative Committee (AALCC) (Manila, March 1996)

Member, Working Group of the ILC on the drafting of the Statute of the International Criminal Court

Member, Drafting Committee of the ILC

Legal expert in a number of Ministerial Committees between Sudan and other countries

Member of the Legal Experts Committee of the Organization of African Unity (OAU), which formulated several regional conventions

Legal adviser in the Ministerial Councils and the Summit Conferences of the OAU (Khartoum, July 1978) (Monrovia, July 1979)

Participant in several meetings and international conferences of WHO, ILO, ITU, WIPO, Red Cross and the Executive Committee of the High Commissioner for Refugees

Member of Special Committees established for fundraising for refugees in Africa

Rapporteur of the Third Committee (Marine Scientific Research) of the summary Ninth session of the

Third UN Conference on the Law of the Sea (Geneva, 1980)

Head of Sudan Delegation to the OAU Preparatory Meeting on the Draft Code of Conduct on Transfer of Technology (Addis Ababa, March 1981)

Spokesman of the African Group and the Group of 77 on all issues pertaining to Transfer of Technology, Energy, Restrictive Business Practices and Technical Co-operation among Developing Countries at the twenty-second and twenty-third sessions of the Trade and Development Board (Geneva, February and September 1981

Head of Sudan Delegation and Spokesman of the African Group and Coordinator of the Group of 77 at the fourth session of the UN Conference on the Code of Conduct on Transfer of Technology (Geneva, March-April 1981)

Spokesman of the Group of 77 on Chapter 9 (Applicable Law and Settlement of Disputes) at the UN Conference on the International Code of Conduct on Transfer of Technology (Geneva, March-April 1981)

Head of Sudan Delegation and Chairman of the Workshop on Legal Policies on Technology Transfer (Kuwait, September 1981)

Chairman of the African Group and the Group of 77 at the first session of the Intergovernmental Group of

Experts on Restrictive Business Practices (Geneva, November 1981)

Chairman of the Permanent Group of 15 on Transfer and Development of Technology, within the United Nations Conference on Trade and Development (UNCTAD) (Geneva, 1980-1983)

Spokesman of the African Group and the Group of 77 at the meeting on the Economic, Commercial and Developmental Aspects of the Industrial Property System (Geneva, February 1982)

Coordinator of the African Group and the Group of 77 at the first, second and third sessions of the Interim Committee on the International Code of Conduct on Transfer of Technology (Geneva, March, May, September-October 1982)

Coordinator of the African Group and the Group of 77 at the Meeting of Governmental Experts on the Transfer, Application and Development of Technology in the Capital Goods and Industrial Machinery Sectors (Geneva, July 1982)

Coordinator and spokesman of the African Group and the Group of 77 at the Intergovernmental Group of Experts on the Feasibility of Measuring Human Resource Flows on Reverse Transfer of Technology (Brain-Drain) (Geneva, August-September 1982)

Coordinator of developing countries on the drafting of the resolution concerning the mandate of the Office of the United Nations High Commissioner for Refugees, during the thirty-third session of the Executive Committee of the UNHCR (Geneva, October 1982)

Coordinator and spokesman of the African Group and the Group of 77 at the Meeting of Governmental Experts on the Transfer, Application and Development of Technology in the Energy Sector (Geneva, October-November 1982)

Coordinator and spokesman of the African Group and the Group of 77 at the fourth session of the Committee on Transfer of Technology (Geneva, November-December 1982)

Member, Board of Patrons, IP Management Resource (On-line version of Intellectual Property/ Innovation Management Handbook), 2007

Co-President, Foreign Relations Committee, Ministry of Culture (Sudan, 2011)

President, Sudan Foundation for the defense of Syrian people (2012-2013)

Vice-President, Sudan Foundation for the defense of Rights and Freedom s (2012-2013)

Member, Sudan Foundation for Reconciliation and Religious co-existence (2012-2013)

Judicial Experience and Professional Membership of Associations

Member of the United Nations International Law Commission (ILC) (1992-1996) and (2000-2001)

Member and Chairman of several legal experts committees established within the OAU

Professor of Public International Law, University of Khartoum , Sudan

Member of the Sudan Bar Association (Khartoum)

Member of the African Jurists Association (Dakar and Paris)

Alternate Chair, Council of Foreign Relations, Ministry of Culture, Sudan

Registered Advocate and Commissioner for Oaths in the Republic of Sudan

Vice President, Sudan Organisation for the Protection of Fundamental Rights and Freedoms

Member, Sudan High Level Committee on Judicial Reform

Projects and Documents

Formulated and negotiated, on behalf of WIPO, numerous projects relating to development cooperation in the field of intellectual property

Organized, on behalf of WIPO, various seminars and workshops and presented several lectures

Drafted various documents on developmental aspects of intellectual property

Supervised and managed the administrative and substantive aspects of projects executed worldwide

Conferences, Seminars, Courses and Symposia

Represented Sudan in numerous international and regional conferences; participated in many seminars, symposia, discussion groups, and addressed graduate students on various international academic disciplines

Represented WIPO, in various international meetings, seminars and symposia

Represented WIPO on several UNDP Policy and Operations Programmes

Undertook a study tour at the Max Planck Institute (Munich) in the field of teaching of intellectual property law (1986)

Extensive lecture on COVID-19: The legal consequences of contractual obligations (May, 2020)

Publications

Euro-Arab Dialogue, June 1977

State Responsibility in International Law, September 1977

The Theory of Human Action, September 1977

The Philosophy of "Haddith" and "Sunna" in Islamic Law, January 1978

The Doctrine of Jurisdiction in International Law, December 1978

American Embassy in Tehran Case, March 1979

The Legal Regime of the Nile, December 1980

Issues pertaining to Transfer and Development of Technology in Sudan, May 1981

China and the Powers in the 19th Century, May 1981

Legal Dimensions of the Economic Cooperation among Developing Countries, June 1981

The Common Fund for Commodities, June 1981

General Aspects of Transfer of Technology at the National and International Levels, November 1981

Preferential Trading Arrangements among Developing Countries, February 1982

North-South Insurance Relations: The Unequal Exchange, December 1984

The Law of Non-Navigational Uses of International Water Courses; the International Law Commission's draft articles: An overview, November 1995

The Theory of Source and Target in Child Psychology, January 1996

A Better United Nations for the New Millennium, January 2000

Intellectual Property – A Power Tool for Economic Growth, 2003

Sudan, The Year 2020: Lessons and Visions, 2004

The Intellectual Property-Conscious Nations: Mapping the Path from Developing to Developed, 2006

Sudan 2020, (2008)

Sudan: From Least-Developed to Fast Developing, 2008

Arbitration: A Vision for the Enforcement of Justice, 2009

Arbitration: Critical Review Of Sudan Legislation onArbitration (2005), 2009

A guide to my philosophy and quotations, 2015

Sudan's Path to the Future: A realistic dream for 2025, 2017

JASTA and the third World War, 2018

A Memoir: My Nile Odyssey, 2019

How: Mind-Set Success, Promise: Nothing Less Than My Dream, 2020

My Nile Odyssey (Arabic translation): 2022

JASTA and the third World War (Arabic translation): 2022

My Nile Odyssey (Audio Book):2023

Books under publication

WHISPERS OF POWER:
ENCOUNTERS WITH GLOBAL ICONS

VOLCANIC FURY:
THE DEADLY TOLL OF ANGER

BEYOND THE VEIL:
A METAPHYSICAL ODYSSEY

SILENT WISDOM:
THE POWER OF SAYING NOTHING

DEMYSTIFY:
The UNSEEN PATH:
Insights from Moses and Al Khidr

UNIVERSE CONTROLLED:
THE SOVREIGNTY OF ALLAH

DARK SECRETS:
The HIDDEN TRUTHS

HEART's THRONE:
WHY THE MIND IS JUST A PUPPET?

Articles

A number of articles on law, economics, jurisprudence and aesthetics published in various newspapers and periodicals.

Russia's Invasion of Crimea: Is it a violation of International Law?

Index

www.ingramcontent.com/pod-product-compliance
Lightning Source LLC
LaVergne TN
LVHW051421080426
835508LV00022B/3188